HE TOLD ME

POEMS
BY
TYLER FRENCH

Published by Capturing Fire Press, Washington, DC

ISBN: 978-1-7328759-3-7

Capturing Fire Press is an independent publishing house founded by
Regie Cabico that seeks to promote politically charged, performance
& experimental poetry of the highest quality by diverse queer poets
from around the globe.

Cover design by Ben Carver, see more at benjamincarver.art

Printed in the United States of America

Table of Contents

I am still grateful to him. I hope he is alive
and may happen to read these lines.
*- **Christopher Isherwood***

Queer Love

*After Eve Kosofsky Sedgwick**

I used to think I fell in love too easily,
as if my heart turned tuning fork
at the smallest sonic suggestion
listen, you can hear it now maybe
listen closely, me falling in love
with readers I will never know
though we will never touch
we know after we finish
our poem we can buy a family-sized
bag of ruffles potato chips and know
that family can mean just me,
or us, or us and your other lovers, and mine too and
friends and their lovers and pushy femmes and radical
fairies and fantasists and drags and clones and leather folk
and ladies in tuxedoes and feminists and masturbators and
bulldaggers and divas and butch bottoms and snap queens*
I know now I was wrong before believing love
was something easy, believing my ringing heart
a cracked and false thing. It is a love that comes
from knowing what it is to want, it is a love
that comes from learning to live without lack.
Your love allows me to be risky with my weight
because our hearts know alarm bells
and birdsong in equal measure.
I used to think I fell in love too easily.

Softie

Broken AC

they are separate
from each other
yet both called
or asked to be
or knew themselves
or didn't know themselves
as *boy*, yet

hands like old envelopes
their glue losing to the humidity
of a late South Carolina
summer baring secrets across
a sheet of shoulder blade
not touching until

> the lights are off
> his leg might
> become his leg
> or his tongue his
> tongue his fingers
> pushed deep inside
> of him or himself or
> both and he worried

about this unfurling
he worried his body
would be lost into
his body but isn't
that what he wanted
all along?

to be lost?

Leftie – Left Hook – Out of Left Field

i bit his leg
rolled through grass
calf in mouth

he was one year older
i was not going to beg
for mercy or a time out

we became grass there
limbs to be mowed
every Saturday

~

how touch turned to tackle

and how tackle could have meant
       flip-flop / hand-offs / going long / buttonhook

skins or shirts

or I'll be shirts
everyone else
skins

~

chased down the block with a golf club
heads teed up, one by one
you don't come back
from that

~

how tackle turned to conquer
how I wanted to be

~

pinned down in the snow
hot breath condensed

in our coat collars
how much that felt like love
and sex i'm still trying
to figure out how to play

our faces red and sweaty
i wouldn't have known
that that was how that worked
then but maybe

i did maybe
he did too

Strapped

Sports Authority aisle 12: suppression shorts,
knee pads and mouth guards, plastic in the mouth
rubber and iron, bloody air fluorescents, then

what we came to buy: white and thick-banded
made for protection, the plastic cup featured
in clear packaging obscuring the package

a protector eventually penetrated by fantasies
cleats, grass stained shorts, open showers, mists
of axe, blood in the mouth, rubber and silicone

furry stomach of the college kid, coach's helper
when he lifted his shirt to wipe his face, so he
couldn't see me see his white band peeking out

They Kept Moving the Flag

sit up / straight / straighten out a spine used to curve / used to
hillock / if I don't / they'll lay the sod over and know me as a mound
/ to trip over

        I beg him to use my c-curve / bone into and then into
/ and then finally soft / and then finally soft enough / I cradle his
skull and warn him / don't try to see me in the stars / they don't give
us constellations

        when the lightning bugs (fireflies?) lit our games of
capture the flag I saw a fox. I saw the fox's eyes first / bone cinder
white / and sat and listened to the other team crack twigs

he's got to be here somewhere

You Gotta Clear the Cookies

crumb trail leading to *I was curious*

    at your age too

dial soap in the bathroom
next to the shared family computer
not-quite-jasmine, greener
with lemon – something *fresh-*

er lily pad, pond scum green
fingers and wet mouth, hard-
wood cabinet and black
desk chair on wheels, quick spin

google searches:
        straight men naked
        masturbation techniques
        sex and…

seeing (green pond) the screen (myself)
and loving that (myself, finally) too much
to be merely curious (at my age too)

It Didn't Last

The first time a boy told me

    you are so soft
his hands on the part of my lower back
that rises over the band of my underwear
like just kneaded dough before proofing

    it doesn't matter
he tells me, he knows,
        even if I'm skin and bones,
        i will always have this soft,
        here.

he says feeling my soft spots
his soft spots pressed against me
    lamb skin gloves, maybe

two soft boiled boys
crack us open and find
our insides still yolky

maybe

nessie the nelly

boy, not loch ness
not monster but
      monster-like

not bottom feeder
but bottom maybe
neck long and slender
like, nessie has a lot to see
has a lot to peer out of
      stereoscope-like

out of dark water
skin, not scales
but skin that must be
      scale-like

always misidentified
maybe eel, seal, shark
or trees, seismic gas
maybe hoax
maybe not boy but
      boy-like

or an optical effect
when you see that swish
you think maybe
monster. you think
maybe mirage.
you think maybe not
      -like.

Role Play

5 Role-Playing Scenarios

1. you: mailman :: me: an orange

Juice me with your mailman thighs
Make me pulp citrus quench queen
Mat the hair curling out of your short brown shorts with sticky juice
Slosh me in your cupped hands
Your cupped hands whose fingers could have ripped open so many
secrets
Whose fingers sting with paper cut
Let them sting a while before slurping me down:
        I am vitamin C
        I am not a cure
Your body will parcel me out
Get rid of the rest
You were never much into piss play
But you'll let me sit in the toilet a while
Before flushing me away
Zip up your shorts
And feel what is left of me on your thigh hairs
In your capacity to be well
And the stinging of your finger tips

2. *you: thumb :: me: forefinger*

We both point in different directions
Me forward, you back
Sometimes so much so
We cleave the web skin between us
Split and crack brittle paper.
Let's rub ourselves smooth with worry instead
Show the world we're more than arch, loop, or whirl.
Together we can make an A-OK
Sometimes my inverse as an occasional bedfellow
To make it that much less wholesome.
       I forget we are of the same blood
We try to feel each other's heartbeats
Which means we try to feel our own
The trick is to press without pressing—
Hold without withholding—
And breathe

3. you: milkmaid :: me: a butter churn

This is our most misunderstood role-play.
It seems easy at first,
You to pump me up and down
But it's more complicated than that.
We are in a historic house museum, it's 2018
There are no cows to be made milk
For butter or worse
You laughed the first time you told that joke
But 127 tour groups later
Your laugh is as empty as I am
As I've been for two centuries.
Your milk white skin now caramel at the end of summer
I watch you change out of your apron
Into blue jeans for the last time
And peel off in your boyfriend's Camaro
Off to school for good.
You touched me once
Even though the curator told you not to touch the objects
The oils on your hand
Sped up my slow decay
And for that
I thank you

4. *you: picnic :: me: watermelon*

But first, would I were the damp earth
For some green thumb to push into
Make me moon with craters
Set inside the seeds I saved in my mouth
To savor the way they sprout into and root out of
Cross vine over limb
My fertile crescent cupped here
Scoop out with paw
Split pulp kidney-red slush
Dig in and scrape the rind with your nails
Mirror the stripe outside
Sing the praises of slurp and gush
Squirt between teeth
Too closely spaced to spit out seed
Don't wipe your lips
Leave your smiles sticky
For me

5. *you: me :: me: somebody's else*

I never meant to write us an elegy
But I did. Sorry.
You'll have to perform acts of self-desiccation
Make yourself like a canyon without its river
And wait for it to rain
This may not seem particularly erotic at first
But you will never feel so much
As when your skin sits this close
To your bones. Wait for it to rain.
I can only guess at the next part
But, know you, although some new river
Will soon flow through your canyon
It will follow the course of your old river
At least at first
Wait for it to rain
And when it does you will once again
Feel that fleshy swell

I promise

Gay Pastoral

I've found myself writing pastoral poems lately,
how he is a county in my mouth.
We have no sovereignty over the meaning described on our bodies
only what we do with them,
which, I think, is also to say *I know my body best*
when it is less my body than someone else's.

My poems may function pastorally, but I hate the outdoors.
Maybe they're not quite as liberated as I would like to think,
maybe it's a self-hatred disguised as metaphor.
My allergies keep me from enjoying the idylls of wheat crop
populating these pages this pleasant summer-sunned recreation:

> pock mark the soil with gripping heal
> and sow into the peat blood cut out
> of tongue through grit teeth.
> We will not treat each other
> like kings in disguise. We are not kings

> in disguise. Although I would have liked to say
> we did. But if we were both kings,
> would we not have known each other as peasants?
> The dirt under my nails isn't so easily
> soaped away as my knees are grass stained.

A beautiful place is not so much a spot on his body
but how I think of that spot on his body
not so much the glass but the fingerprints you leave there
not so much the fingerprints but the sun shining through them
not so much the sun but the motes of pollen in that sun's shine
whisked away on a bee's legs

I never gave myself the ability to know another's body innocently.
When our countries met, we were way past oral
eager to give head, how you smiled up at me
how pleased you were leading me cock in mouth
to another greener knoll.

Even in poems wiped clean of "I"
don't forget this poet knows how to lead
as well as be led. To beam
with the joy of giving such pleasure
two pastors out to pasture to chew cud
the matted grass of our love disordered linen.

When I say his ass is hillock
what I mean it that it is mountable
not mountain. That it is grass not hard rock.
His country is one I know as well as my own
but inversely, I feel it but will never feel it myself
and that is what we mean by sovereign:

      your loam mildly loathsome, but
      let me know the mud of you
      let me taste the terroir of your homeland
      to gauge its salinity against my own
      to know where you have been weary traveler
      before my country.

      We won't shower until after
      until we've had our fill of this foreign
      and then we can be renewed fields
      for a while together.
      If only a short while.

Orange Peel

Dishwash hands capped with drip-dried nailpolish
    you swish the dishwater dirty again.

Insert nail here, peel back the skin and
    scrape away the peal of a lover's laugh.

Your hands will smell navel all day
    fingers ending abruptly in peeling orange.

Glass Bird

There are many things that have yet to make themselves clear to me
& there are walls of glass at right angles to each other, forming a
house, there are the prints of my two cupped hands, wrapped around
my eyes rapt & there's you, reflected, stepping out of the shower,
your chest hair dew covered, taken from a cowslip's ear &

I hear a plane fly by, low, the airport's near. How much does it take
to get to Venice? *You'd like it there* I fog the glass, I fog the glass so
that if I were a bird, I would know when to stop &
you've windexed the shit out of this & if you were a bird you wouldn't
know when to stop & I lean too far in &

I crash through, hands bleeding, face bleeding & you lean too hard
against the glass & find yourself inside. *My mother had a glass heart, my
father, a glass jaw,* you say, plucking out the shards of the windows of
your house, of glass so like yourself, I can't help running my palms
together now to feel the scars, to feel if there are still any pieces of
you left under my skin.

I polish you every day after I crash through, I polish you to blind
those outside of our vacation, to blind those outside of this gondola
with rainbows, with carnival masks & Titian clouds reflected in your
face & there are souvenir glass birds, palm-sized finches, slightly blue,
blown before our eyes, red hot, coal fired & I ask *Was that what it was
like? Being red hot, then coal fired?* We don't talk until I come back with a
cup of molten sand & there are thousands of shattered faces back
and forth reflected from cup to lips to cup to brow to cup to cheek
to cup to the bird you hold up dripping with molten sand.

As you unpack I fire through the pantry looking for something to eat.
I round the corner & call your name, throwing it like a rock & there
is your answer, a twinned response from the twinkle of the crystal
chandelier. There are constellations stuck into the carpet & into &
out of my shins & there is your nose, a crunch under my bare feet.
Then the hush of cut glass cracking light & rainbows on the white
walls &

there is the broom I used to sweep away the rest of you. There I find the glass bird in our suitcase, complete, completely there, unbroken even after the long flight. I polish the bird clear, careful to not etch it with my splintered digits.

Domestic Me

Do-   mes-
tic   me.
Do   me
ec-   sta-
tic-   ally.
Do   *Re*
Me.   Be
fath-   er-
less   to
me,   lest
you   make
me   call
you   dad-
dy.   Me,
son   or
mom-   my
or   dad-
dy   too.

The Etiology of the Warbler

It starts with

The Story of a Boy Who Caught a Frog in his Throat
How it croaked
and stretched long legs
made this boy's Adam's apple bigger than the rest.
He would sleep with his mouth open
so the frog could catch flies
until one day that story met

The Story of a Boy Who Could Turn Frogs into Birds
The two boys woke together bed-headed at sunrise marked by chirp
until one day that chirp changed
grew louder and more distinct
the bird worried its way out of the boy's throat
and flew away.
Birds fly away, their fathers had told them, before a drought
so the conjurer-boy stripped and reclined in that last big rain
he collected it in the concavity of his breastbone—
he held more there than his heart—
and thus began

The Story of a Boy Who Became a Rain Catcher
The first boy carried water in his mouth to the Rain Catcher's lips
until one day his lips became veined stone.
They spoke in waterfalls
and intoned rainbows when the clouds parted.
They had to sit very still
so as not to upset the lore of the boy's sternum
and spill the water they had stored there
so they told each other stories to wait out the drought
and ate morsels of truth
and more toothsome mouthfuls of fib
they gnawed on tales older than they were tall
letting them soften in their cheeks before attempting to chew
sinewy morals stuck close to their gums.
First the insects came
then small fowl followed soon after
rodents, reptiles, antlered deer
fauna, flora, from far and near
caught wind of this oasis
to drink the water, sweet and clear.
Brought by the boys' just-so stories,
mothers filled their clay jugs at the lip of their ribs.
They rubbed the boys' feet for thanks.
There's a saying that it takes three men to make a tiger
yet these two lost boys found each other and made an empire.
The pool grew larger as more used it
some inner spring welling up so big
the first boy had to cradle the Rain Catcher in his thighs

The Story of a Mountain and a Lake
These boys became kings clothed as forest
until one day Spring grew up and around their girth
their skin at the water's edge smooth rock
shoulder blades cliffs
and fingers gripped deep in dirt to root the precious azure.
Finally, the drought ended
and the frog that was a bird flew back.
It couldn't find its boy so it perched on the lip of a damp cave.
It felt like home, but it wasn't.

The Story of a Frog Who Still Waits for His Prince
Greeting the towheaded dawn with his mourning warble

Dismal Americana

I feel abject   and queenly
holey socks and scepter horn rimmed and horny
rollick and roll   slicked back ducktail, cowlicked
I smell green grass   woozy greaseball
come on baby   bobby sock it over here
sit on my knee and tell me, *What do you have to feel queenly about?*

I can be your throne, put my hands on your head for a crown
gold leaf my knees for your hands to rest on, to rub green
you told me you feel faggy and I think I know what you mean
I'll tuck that sour in the corner of my cheek til it tastes sweet for you

I'll swizzle stick you between my lips like paper straw boys who slurp
up milkshakes at the corner drugstore, we'll twist up like a
barbershop pole, modern day princes trading velvet for leather, and
in the bedroom, leather for more leather

it snaps when you walk
the crease where your butt cheek meets your thigh
popping pink bubblegum blow bubbles for me
stick your wads of chewed rubber to my soles
stick me down to the pavement
I can be the lightning rod to your electric tongue

we'll ride tops down, nipples pointing North, wind comb back our
hair and brush out the pine needles we had stuck there from our
midnight wood. In this Technicolor rework, we can flounce
fearlessly, use our knowledge of fixing muscle cars for tuning up each
other's engines with grease under our nails and handkerchiefs tied
twice over our eyes.

We are Americana's dismal royalty. That sour in my cheek will only
taste sweet when we learn to laugh at ourselves along with them.

So come on baby   bobby sock it over here
sit on my knee and tell me, *What do you not have to feel queenly about?*

Sexual Practice

A Mean Chillicothe Winter

you said *you are thoroughly Midwestern*
with a heart not corn fed but sprouts
corn silk Ohio sky blue eyes
& slow…
I'm not from the Midwest but half my family
is doilies and draped blankets
the mantel held down by trinkets and dust
woozy floorboards
maybe you meant old fashioned
did caring go out of vogue?
maybe it's cupping the silence between us
reducing it down
condensed & corn syrupy
pressing it until I can coat myself
the way you wear it so plainly yourself
maybe it's an overblown superstition
when I texted twice in a row
or how I can't hide my blush
when I mispronounce pinot grigio
maybe it's too much eye contact
you're just so nice
maybe you could run rings with your fingers
round all my joints, remind me how to be
soft cornered and hearth-hearted
I had forgotten my love
is losing fingerprints to the brownie pan
because I didn't use the oven mitts
because I didn't want them to burn
pushing my chair in after dinner
and twirling your toe knuckle hair
I had forgotten at least
half of my love might be
too much
for you

Total Eclipse 2017

When I opened Grindr
in the eclipse's path of totality
the display names listed:

in the area
just lookin
or *seeing whats around*

in this moment of bodies aligning
remembering these bodies are celestial too
at least at our origin points

empirically speaking we are star stuff
learning Rick liked to have his nipples licked
Stephan just wanted to cuddle

and someone whose name I never learned
wanted to hold me down I wanted him
to hold me down to smother me make me feel
less like myself the way a body might feel
in the dark lose its shape at its edges

in the dark of the eclipse, a temporary dark
the shadows didn't have the chance to get long
it wasn't a proper night

there was no need for me to feel so alone
the sun was playing a kind of trick
a disappearing act

knowing then more than ever
that I wasn't a scientist
I never felt more like a poet,

I never felt more sick of this act
having friends who've tried it out themselves
except they didn't come back

and they've left this kind of outline
and when I can take off those stupid glasses
and finally look all I can see is nothing

what's the point of trying to look at stars
if our eyes aren't able to see them
I could never know the sun better
than when it's negated
in this moment of bodies aligning

remembering these bodies are celestial too
when I opened Grindr and he asked if I was looking
I said, *yes just looking*

An Ode to Crabs

After Sharron Olds

O, lil QTs be glad I am a sadomasochist
because I enjoyed the burn you gave me
how your itch kept me company longer
than he did, a summer romance to end all
summer romances of little fruit tarts
and shorter swimming suits and bronzed thighs
you came under the guise of an evening
in the grass watching *Clueless* with A.
posed as an innocent allergic reaction before
I'd gotten a closer look and you revealed
your horrific acrobatics under a lamp
on my bedside table, you tiny translucent
crustaceans trapeze-ing around in my crotch
I do not know how I would mistake you
Pediculus Pubis, O bloody sweet teeth,
all my moles looked like your nits
I'd try to scape them off only to find
they were me, peel back my skin and find
I'm not tangerine, pineapple, kiwi,
mango, no more like apple, homegrown
pesticide-free no more, you sycophantic
nymphs made me revoke my all natural
license, the lice killing shampoo
was not gentle on either of us
I said a thousand thanks as I combed
your poisoned husks out of my pubes
Thank you, crystalline parasites
had I never looked so closely at my skin,
I wouldn't have learned that sometimes
it's better to spend a summer alone
by the pool in your cute new suit
than it is to pretend you like someone enough
to believe them when they told you
they didn't know

Sexual Practice 1

he eats
an orange
thumbs me
       open
splits me
not quite
in the middle
rips apart
peel still
connected
to flesh
sprays me
across the table
licks his
forearm
hair sticky

Sexual Practice 2

instead of fisting
we are into heading
also known as un-

mothering
are you my mother?

when I touch your nipples
I wouldn't be surprised
if you milked me instead

Sexual Practice 3

make a trough
of your body

spill leftovers into
and gobble them up

your little piggy's pink
curly Q wriggling

with pleasure
I don't oink

for anyone else

Smoking Weed After a Nice Dinner Out (w/ Three V Expensive Margaritas), But Before You Told Me You Didn't Want a Boyfriend

I had a great time

leave the grass long behind this Georgetown row house, leave me something to hold onto, because we know digging fingers into the dirt never works, we know you need the give of long grass to get that good sway

I've totally become a runner since moving to DC

piles of dirty laundry on the rented basement carpet, begging to be yelled at, the heavy black button down he gave me, trace the heart with his grandmother's name on his shoulder, such a good boy, sweet like hay

but

played "These Days" by Nico on his macbook and rolled me around in his desk chair, in his lap, fingers in the long grass of my chest hair, newly long, only then curling, still very green, an indigo haze blanketing his twin bed

I am totally a bottom

Starbucks the next morning tastes rusty iron scythe as his sweet ran away and I waited for the circulator bus

you can have it

riding another bus, a train, to VA where it is more green, where they were mowing outside my apartment, spring onions and dandelions, a whirring, I could see the earth's bald spots

you'll feel it
if you hold it inside longer

Clockmaker

He is a clockmaker but
my heart is not a clock

My heart is not a clock but
it does keep time steadily

It does keep time steadily but
for this moment it stutters

For this moment it stutters but
the blue blood, it clots

The blue blood, it clots but
still the last pulse in my fingers

Still the last pulse in my fingers but
I am let out, as if leech-covered

I am let out, as if leech-covered but
barely pink (and black and blue)

Barely pink (and black and blue) but
not warm. You only know gears

Not warm. You only know gears but
your father was a doctor

Your father was a doctor but
you were a clockmaker

You were a clockmaker but
my heart was not a clock.

Sadsub™

Chatrandom Boys
would like access
to your webcam + mic
click *Accept*

click *Next* to find
a man with a beard
preferably gray to match
the robe I'm wearing

uncover my thighs, touch
closer to the backs of my knees
the part of my legs I hated
the soft parts

the parts I sometimes pinch
and don't feel anything
but others' fingernails brush
electric hush + hum

I'm developing, I tell him, the role of a depressed submissive partner,
Sadsub™, *Sadsub™* lies in this robe and you lie on top of me and
reach into my mouth with your fat fingers, find the bull vertebrae and
pull, find this *Sadsub's™* affinities with earthworm, jellyfish, spineless
things, easy to squish I've been crying a lot recently and I don't know
how to right this body, I mean write beyond this body, I mean...we
would play this game, my cousins and I, one of us would lie in the
crook of the couch, we would cover each other with pillows and
blankets and cushions and take turns using the mound as a
somersault hill, a punching bag, a landing pad I remember not being
able to breathe, being pressed flat by their percussive leaps, their
elbows, knees, and giggles softened by the mound above to dull
thuds and gray noise, only weight compressing the small pocket of air
between mouth and flannel blanket and when does this desire to be
depressed I mean to be pressed into the mattress overwhelm me or
my ability to say no? When you press me flat between two screens I
might not be able to cry anymore –

he clicked *Next*
leaving me
finding new partner
I close *Chatrandom Boys*

but leave my cam on
not to watch myself doing it
but to feel like someone is
I name the parts I like

willing someone else
to name them like that
start at the soft spots
inside my thighs

closer to the backs of my knees
the part of my legs I hated
And the screen is full of me touching my soft parts
And the screen is full of me watching myself touch my soft parts

He told me

He told me he'd like me to fuck him on the set of Bambi. And I blushed and fawned,

>*I guess we all have mommy issues.*

Let me back up.

He told me he'd like to make love on the set of Bambi, but we'd make the set first ourselves of paper mâché illusions. In this false spring

>*We could get all twitterpatted* said the owl.
>*It could happen to you* said the owl.

The story of a deer who learns that love means many things to many people. I forgot it was about love and how brown and gray that love looks now. Our set would be brighter. Our memory of the movie cutting out the love interests,

I'd nickname him Thumper

he'd call me Bambi, somehow more feminine now that we forgot Faline,
>recast her as the breeze,

I'm more doe-eyed, nuzzled into Thumper's fur, my long tongue wanting salt lick. He'd teach me how to make that tongue wrap itself around syllables more saccharine than salty, more of spring's sweat than summer's

Bur. Say, "Bir-duh!" *Bir-duhhh. Butterfly. Flower. Purty Flower.*

Afterwards wrap me up in the backdrop, cuddle me inside trees, lose each other in the flat foliage, Astroturf, and bulbs blazing above.

A Way Through

The Grand March of Fruits

After "A Supermarket in California" by Allen Ginsberg

Great Uncle Allen watching Great-Great Uncle Walt, you were never so avuncular checking out the heads of cabbage, rosying their cheeks with your dirty fingernails grown long in death.

Would you recognize my America? Now your beard is so long, but you are so thin. I'd like to nurse your hairy skeleton back to life 'til you were once again the full-bodied bear of American poetry you always were. Tell Walt, beards are back now. You'd both fit right in.

More or less aberrant trio we, not so abnormal as strawberries in the dead of winter, but so much more sweet. A whole parade of fruits separates us. Would you know how to eat a kiwi? Would I be one of your grocery boys? Who are your Angel?

How much free use would you two have made of Costco sample day? What America of love have we lost? What is more American love than cheap hospitality, freely given, but only if it's ready in minutes?

Or would I be the store detective? I didn't know you were queer the first time I read your poems, but I felt it queerly. Allen, would you think me queer here with that husband's husband scanning barcodes in the self-checkout line? Would you know me queer the way I knew you two? I take all your books to bed with me, tuck me into the tomatoes—a fruit, remember—and let your words be my lullaby.

So I Guess We Never Came

We were stuck in this eternal return of *could not* and *was not ad infinitum*
and yet, there is no return now, of your body to mine, at least not as
of the writing of this & when your dog licked my foot, I thought that
might have meant return, or at least a before and if not

a before (there was not a before), at least an after & my knees clicked
when I was on all fours on your bed like our teeth clicked around
tongues & your dog tongued the sole of my right foot & my sore
throat the next day said chlamydia, clam up, chowder head

tennis elbow, the smell of a fresh can of tennis balls, your balls (I
can't remember them but as tennis balls, how horrific), Tammi
caught me on the way home, they had just been lube wrestling so we
slicked right off each other, but I got their Instagram handle & they
followed me back

I wipe the lube off my phone screen the next morning, you
recognized my tattoo, Sabina's bowler hat, not Magritte's like
everyone else thinks, I am no apple to take a bite out of, I don't
know how you might take knowledge from this body when I hardly
know it

myself, but that's a fib & that is why I wanted you on top of me,
imagining that weight & warm can approximate return, I feel so
stupid calling it that b/c when you spent on top of me, I felt
expensive and expendable, you don't need a Kleenex

as you milk the last of it out, wipe on my chest and dismount, fast
enough to not get stuck to me, the ungluing of semen crusted pubes,
sadistic Velcro, we didn't quite give each other tennis elbow getting
there,

to here, to cleaning off in the shower, sweeping me down the stairs &
asking for a copy of a poem & it was actually pretty good for a
Grindr hookup & we will still text I guess, but when I get home

I lie on the floor b/c it's too hot outside, I say, but it's really so I can send suggestive Snapchats, what is today's confessional poem when I get stuck in the eternal return of Facebook Instagram Grindr Snapchat Scruff Tumblr (I don't have a Twitter)

swiping past another inflatable unicorn in the pool of #instagay #summer #woof & if one thing is true, you really are beautiful & if only one thing can be true, that should be enough

I Hope It Comes Swiftly

& if not swiftly
I hope it comes
quietly at least
& if not quietly
at least I'll have
learned by this
point not to pull
my thigh away
when I see it
on the screen
up there &
all of my holes
will open
as in yes
as in
please
remembering
the eyes
are holes
too

You told me to spit in your mouth

so I spit in your mouth.

You told me to spit in your mouth again
so I spit in your mouth again
and I kept spitting in your mouth
until you were the Atlantic Ocean

and I kept spitting in your mouth
until you were the Pacific,
then you were all the oceans
and all the oceans rising

(because our bedroom isn't cut
off from the effects of climate change)
and you took out Venice for drinks,
covered New York in your booty wave

and I kept spitting in your mouth
until you became The Flood
like the last flood, "the flood,"
Noah's flood was only practice

for *The Flood*, you: flood
and only then you closed
your mouth so I stopped spitting
and we kissed and I tasted flood.

I tasted all the bodies, salt and fresh
as one body of water in one body
and that might be what drowning is
like, kissing a flood and then coming

up for air, then deciding to dive in again
and it reminded me to never underestimate
the power we have, one boy spitting
into another boy, to fill him up

and be made full himself

A Taxonomy in Providence, RI

you were telling me about flowers because I didn't know
any of their names every blue one *bluebell* every crinoline

carnation & you were telling me those "bluebells" growing
waist high out of the sidewalk were called *chicory* & how

they turn brown when you pick them & that is why they get
so high no one wants a vase of brown flowers & once

you told me my heart was like sunshine & honey & I thought
that's much to sweet to write in a poem I thought about *sunshine*

& *honey* & how my heart could be something that is in part made
by itself I thought I would have to apologize for writing something

so sweet in a poem I thought I would have to apologize for the
desires of this skin again & again & if I tell you I am an uptight *peony*

would you know what I meant? If I gave you a bouquet of crimson
fuckwad sweating *rhododendron* & *rose thorns* would you know

what I meant? If I picked you a bunch of *bluebells* would you
set them in your grandmother's porcelain vase the same

as any other flower whose name I'll never remember?

Empty Apartments in Orlando

we live our lives
in the middle of things

heart-shaped shells, magnets
rings, postcards, so-so ties,
miniatures packed away

cardboard boxes, taped shut
neatly stacked by the door
wait for the moving van to come

to the apartments of those who didn't get home
that night – that night which bled into morning –
these apartments up for rent now

his keys there by the door
he didn't get to realize he'd locked himself
out, he was already late to the party

she never dusted, the blinds thick
with it, bunnies roll out from under the bed
monsters of nothing but what we leave behind

we live our lives in the middle
of things

their bed was still made – the sheets
would have been rumbled by writhing bodies
pleasure soaking through the mattress

losing our lives in the middle of things

we are no strangers to disaster
the joy of leaving behind the things
whose loss is no disaster:

heart-shaped shells, magnets
rings, postcards, so-so ties
miniatures packed away

the dildo collection, his friend, a sister,
this angel packed them up first
before the other family arrived

a laugh when he sticks the big one
to the fridge, the head heavy, it bobs,
his laugh short, but a laugh,

a moment of breath lost to a smile instead
its peel, the rotten orange he finds
in the bottom drawer of the fridge

we live our lives in the middle of things

wilted greens, spoiled
milk, funky yogurt,
trash bags full of food

a t-shirt with holes in the pits
the smell of him around the collars
dirty laundry piles, a deflated boy

the lipstick stained coffee cup
they bought on vacation
its vista now more developed

fingers through brushed wigs
the box fan blows the red one
and she is alive again for that swish

there in the middle of things

we live
our lives

Walking Lucas On a Farm in Jamestown, RI

The goats gathered together at dusk
and faced us in a cluster, a trip
of horned and hooved stone-still
except for their mouths, chewing

in formation. Where we saw an omen,
a 13-headed horror sculpted for us,
Lucas wagged his tail, leapt forward
and yipped, crushing the dandelions.

Back in the city, when we walk him
all of the neighbors call from their stoops
while he shits under the cherry tree
and we gather it in the biodegrable baggies.

They call out, he's getting slower isn't he?
He crushes the dandelions and yips and we follow.

P-town, June 25, 2018

I was gelling my hair the morning before mounting the Pilgrim's
Memorial Monument
and I found a strand of yours in the blue goop, I wasn't able to pluck
it out so I slicked

the gel through my hair, forward from the back then up in the front
and up again
and your black clipping was stuck in my cowlick for the day, I know it
fell out

from a spot on your head I can see from behind, I've never told you
that, and when I am behind
and inside, I try not to pull too hard on your hair, even when you ask
me to pull

harder, when you give fully, I read the monument was erected in 1907,
to give
remembrance to the first landing of the Pilgrims, an ancestor of mine
was there,

and I climb to the top with you pasted to my head and I imagine you
laughing
when I joke I'm going to jump, I'm sooo over this phallic nostalgia,
these ghost boners, bloody

and bloodless staircases to what, God? The Heavens? Closer to the
Clouds? You
told me you lost your body once, after we came, poppers on the sheets,
and as you towel off

in the hallway I clean your hair out of the drain, tuck it into the silver
trashcan and we check
Scruff to confirm we both still enjoy and have had enough of it too,
8.5", rok solid, vers

tops, anyways you weren't here to put sunscreen on my back at the Tea
Dance
so I asked big gay Duke to do it for me and I giggled like the fern we
bought from the

Home Depot does when the AC kicks on when he squirted on my
back, and if I don't die
from jumping (joking) I might from melanoma or the flight home or
Lyme disease, the ticks

at the beach were vicious, honey, because I know my body will give
first, ultimately
and when you read this poem, you will say, Fuck you, Tyler! My hair
isn't falling out!

and then we will have sex, because we haven't seen each other for a
while, and that
is what we do and you will remind me how I don't know anything
about the body and

because I am marrying (ha!) a dancer I should grasp how little poets
know about the body,
the actual body, and its limits, how I have to tender your torn abductor
over your head years

after it giving, how the arch of the tongue remembers that of the foot
and how the pelvic floor
mirrors the ceiling of the throat and how your body continues to give
to me,

how easy you make it look, this giving, a dam to a flood or a stone wall
tumbling or the dunes
out here, how you willfully unwill the walls of yourself, how your body
gives makes me want

a different kind of memorial, for us, for our kind, not a tower or a
place to jump from,
but a hole, an opening, a way through.

ACKNOWLEDGEMENTS

This book and many of these poems would not exist without Regie Cabico. I met Regie as a lowly intern, helping produce Capturing Fire: International Queer Summit and Slam in 2014. The poets who Regie brings together to "go in" on the Capturing Fire stage opened up the possibilities of poetry for me. Poetry can be sexy and strange and deeply personal while gesturing to shared experience. It can articulate LGBTQIA+ identities and experience while muddying those articulations, making space for queer joy and solidarity. I am honored to be included in the slate of books published by Capturing Fire Press. Regie and Sasha Sinclair, with Capturing Fire Press, have extended the work of Capturing Fire in exciting ways, further supporting queer poets and producing beautiful anthologies. Thank you to every poet who has attended and supported Capturing Fire. I hear reverberations of your poems and voices in this collection and I look forward to reconnecting every year.

Split This Rock similarly plays a significant role in these poems. The open mic at their 2014 festival was the first time I had read any of my poetry in public. I read a poem, which has since been cannibalized into a number of poems in this book, that scared me and felt nothing but held and supported by the space they stewarded (it was not a very good poem). Split This Rock brings together a beloved community of socially engaged poets whose work asks all of us to write fiercely, as a part of the world around us, using our poetry to pay witness to injustice as well as create a new, more just worlds. Thank you to the Split This Rock staff and friends, Sarah Browning, Camisha Jones, Rasha Abdulhadi, Emma Bartley, M.F. Simone Roberts, and Chelsea Iorlano for the enormous amount of work you do.

Thank you to the readers of early drafts of this book, Clay Mettens (reader of an early, early draft), Briana Mawby, Anna Hicken, Douglas Robson, Alan Siero, Angelique Palmer, Sarah Browning, and Matthew Cumbie (more thanks for you later). Briana, thank you for gifting me the absolute perfect description of the book too! I have such gratitude for every reader and workshoper of individual poems, Simone, Emma, and Camisha, among others. Maggie Goddard, thank you for your thoughts and edits, as well as every conversation, every glass of wine, and for including me as a reader of your work.

Ben Carver, your cover design brought out an aspect of the poems I had forgotten. Thank you for pulling together a design that surprised me and for flirting with me with your camera.

This book extends from a constellation of people too numerous to name, count, or know. Every workshop participant, every open mic reader and audience member, and every slam poet I've shared space with over the past five years have fed these poems. A full list would be another book's worth of characters, but here are a few. Thank you Providence, RI crew, for showing up and holding space, Kara Lynn Noto, Leah Burgin, Andrea Ledesma, Inge Zwart, Emily Sellon, Arielle Julie Brown, Katie Vogel, Jonathan Cortez, Micah Salkind, Teddy McGuire, Sarah Wilbur, Jori Ketten, and 186 Carpenter artists. Thank you DC crew, Alison Whyte, Aditi Dussault, Lee Ann Brantley, Adam Johnston, and Joe Gizzi. Thank you Craig Morgan Teicher and fellow workshop participants at the Fine Arts Work Center in Provincetown, MA (thank you to the Fine Arts Work Center and Split This Rock for the scholarship that allowed my participation). Thank you *Growing Our Own Gardens* cast for demonstrating what queer love might look like in the body, in practice: Darryl Pilate, Juliana Ponguta, Elizabeth Johnson, Samuel Horning, Andy Torres, Michelé Prince, Micah, and Heather Doyle. I miss moving with all of you every day.

Finally, Matthew Cumbie. Thank you for showing up to every open mic, offering first ears to every fledgling poem, every rewrite, and rewrite of every rewrite...I've been called a writer of love poems, but joke that I had never written any poems about you, except that last one. I have since realized that all of the poetry I have written since we met is about you, is made possible by you. This isn't to say I wouldn't be writing poetry if I hadn't met you (yuck). Rather your commitment to artmaking that is connected to lived experience, the queer family you have brought me into, and your own work around queer worldmaking influences and animates my writing. The poems coagulate as extensions of our conversations, responses to your dances, or observations on what constitutes the collaborative acts of holding our lives together, resonant and tenderly. Thank you for being a partner in uncountable ways.

About the author

photo by Ben Carver

Tyler French is a writer, organizer, and public humanist living in Washington, D.C. He works in the arts and cultural non-profit world and writes about the arts and equitable community development. He is a co-creator and baker for Queer Cookies, a poetry series and bake sale supporting queer-identified poets. He has poems in Assaracus: A Journal of Gay Poetry, Beech Street Review, and Bending Genres Journal. See more of his work at tylerhfrench.com. When not writing, he's dancing with his partner, Matthew Cumbie, and cohabitating with a 13-year old shih tzu named Lucas.

www.ingramcontent.com/pod-product-compliance
Lightning Source LLC
Chambersburg PA
CBHW060424050426
42449CB00009B/2114